When Dorothy M. Stewart's husband lobe dementia in 2007, she became his s One Day at a Time: Meditations for Ca 2010, is the fruit of those years. However, as her health gave way and her husband's condition deteriorated, it became time for him to move to residential care. This book is the result. A lay preacher serving ecumenically in Suffolk and Norfolk, Dorothy has a solid foundation in communicating the word of God to encourage, support and strengthen others.

She has had a career in book publishing, at Ahmadu Bello University Press (northern Nigeria), Macmillan Press, McGraw-Hill, Chartac Books (the publishing arm of the Institute of Chartered Accountants in England and Wales) and SPCK.

She has also had a number of books published: *Bluff Your Way in Publishing* (Ravette), *Women of Prayer* (Lion and Loyola), *Women of Spirit* (Lion and Loyola), *The Gower Handbook of Management Skills* (Gower/Ashgate), *The Westminster Collection of Christian Prayers* (Westminster John Knox Press), *It's Hard to Hurry When You're a Snail* (Lion), *A Book of Graces* (SPCK) and *Prayers for the Night* (SPCK). She is an enthusiastic blogger (<dorothystewartblog.wordpress.com>).

STILL CARING

Christian meditations and prayers

Dorothy M. Stewart

First published in Great Britain in 2013

Society for Promoting Christian Knowledge
36 Causton Street
London SW1P 4ST
www.spckpublishing.co.uk

British Library Cataloguing-in-Publication Data
A catalogue record for this book is available from the British Library

ISBN 978–0–281–06983–5
eBook ISBN 978–0–281–06984–2

Typeset by Graphicraft Limited, Hong Kong
First printed in Great Britain by Ashford Colour Press
Subsequently digitally printed in Great Britain

eBook by Graphicraft Limited, Hong Kong

Produced on paper from sustainable forests

Contents

Contents

Acknowledgements

One evening at church, I noticed that a friend was weeping. She had been having a really rough time trying to care at home for her husband after a spell in hospital. Now she was at the end of her tether and struggling with the first few weeks when he had moved to a residential care facility.

My heart went out to her. I wished I could just provide jump leads from my heart and mind to hers so she could absorb all I had learned so she would know, really know, how to manage. And that's when this book was born – for Jenny and for all those in the same situation.

During the writing, I've been supported by the Association of Christian Writers, most specifically by the past chair, Lin Ball, and the present, Mel Menzies, and the ACW Facebook community. I've benefited greatly from the kind and encouraging comments on my Friday and Saturday Dementia Diaries on my blog <www.dorothystewartblog. wordpress.com> and the support and sense of not being alone engendered by the large and lively carers/dementia community on Twitter.

Living alone while a husband or loved one is in a care home can be lonely and tough, but thanks to Facebook and Twitter, you don't ever have to feel isolated! Thank you all.

Introduction

I wrote *One Day at a Time* when I was relatively new to the business of caring at home for someone with dementia. Unable to find any Christian material to help me, I found myself writing my own and it seems to have helped others in the same position.

But now we've moved on and this book is written, once more, out of my own experience and that of friends in the same situation – and for them and those many others with loved ones in residential care. According to the Care Quality Commission (2011), there are 4,608 care homes in the UK offering nursing care and 13,475 that offer residential care without nursing. According to the Association for Children's Palliative Care (ACT), there are more than 23,000 children with life-limiting or life-threatening illness in the UK with approximately 80,000–100,000 family members and carers involved. Add up the numbers and that's a lot of people.

It's clear that many folk have moved on from the care-at-home situation we addressed in *One Day at a Time* and are now struggling and hurting, trying to cope with the upset of having a loved one in a residential/care home. Even where a loved one requires residential care on a temporary basis, whether as respite or for medical reasons, the carer/partner/parent/child will encounter many of the feelings and struggles of the carer whose loved one has moved into permanent care.

This sequel to *One Day at a Time* aims to cover the next stages in the experience of the carer where a loved one needs more care than can be provided at home. The first part of the book (Chapters 1 to 12) deals with the emotional and spiritual wrestling the carer experiences, as well as the practical problems they encounter, in considering residential care. Chapters 13 to 24 tackle the emotional ups and downs of the settling-in period following their loved one's move to residential care, and the biggest bugbear of all: guilt. Chapters 25 to 38 cover the day-to-day readjustments and experiences of having someone living in residential care.

As before, each chapter begins with a short Bible reading, centres on a meditation dealing with that aspect of the situation, and closes with a brief prayer, and a self-care suggestion.

The aim is to support, encourage, reassure, comfort and strengthen family and friends of people in residential care. Though it is based on my own experience, I hope readers will find much to identify with, some things to groan with me at and even some to laugh at. I pray that God will use this book to help many. May God bless you.

STILL CARING

1

Is it time?

There is a time for everything, and a season for every activity under the heavens.   (Ecclesiastes 3.1)

We struggle with this. We've been struggling with all of this caring business for a long time and this, one more decision, looms over us as the almost impossible one. Because how could we? How could we give up and shunt our loved ones off to be looked after by other people, away from their familiar surroundings, away from *us*!

It feels like failure. Defeat. But if we've got to the stage where we've been thinking about it seriously, praying about it, then we've probably been feeling defeated for a while.

'Hand it over to the Lord,' our kind, well-intentioned friends tell us. And we want to point out (isn't that a polite way of saying it!) that we have, we are – but we're still not sure.

'About what?' they ask. 'Isn't it obvious?' Because they can see that we're exhausted, grey in the face, trembly, on the verge of tears – or however 'too much, too long' affects us.

Yes, we know. But we still feel *responsible*. The person involved is *our* mum or dad, *our* spouse, *our* child. It's our job. Nobody else's.

'But you're killing yourself,' they say. 'What good will you be to him dead?' (I am so grateful for my blunter friends who talk fierce good sense to me – the truth in love!) And they remind me of the instructions in the aeroplane about taking down your own oxygen mask first before fitting the one on the person next to you.

Yes. We know. We know all the arguments off by heart – because we're not going into this lightly. We've been over it and over it in our hearts and heads and before the Lord for a long time now. But we still have no answer. We are still asking, 'Is it time?'

Prayer

Loving Lord Jesus, give me your peace in my heart and your wisdom as I struggle to make the best decisions I can for my loved one. I want only to do what is best for him/her and right in your sight. Guide me, I pray.

Self-care suggestion

Get outside for even a moment. If it's raining, just stand by an open door or window – and breathe! Breathe in deep down to the bottom of your lungs. Blow the air out of your mouth. Do it a couple of times, until you feel a bit better. Give yourself time to feel that refreshing cool air filling you and think of the Spirit of God who also fills you and promises to be your Counsellor.

2

There's only me

———•••———

I am the only one left.   (1 Kings 19.10b)

Burn-out. We all know about that. I reckon carers live teetering on the edge of burn-out most of the time, and tipped over the edge into full-on burn-out rather a lot of the time.

It goes with the territory. Right?

I wonder. Reading today's text and the story that goes with it brought me up to a sudden crunch. It seems to me that I and other carers have a tendency to battle on in our own strength and on our own a lot of the time.

Have you ever heard yourself say (possibly crossly), 'Well, there's only me! Who else is there to do it?'

Elijah told God, 'And I only I am left' (to carry on the work).

Yes, that's how it feels. And it's often how we operate, shouldering the whole weight of our situation.

Worse, we can feel that we're the only people who know how to do things the right way, the way our loved ones like or need. Only our way is the right way.

And that sets us up for burn-out. Because if it's true, that we're the only ones who know, the only ones who can do things right . . . then we are indeed indispensable. We genuinely cannot take time off. We have to be there, seeing to everything, night and day.

God told Elijah he'd got it wrong. In fact, God had another bunch of people waiting in the wings to take over. Elijah needed a less self-centred perspective.

Oh yes, I wrote 'self-centred' because that's where Elijah was, doing things the way he thought they should be, telling it how it looked to him. And God had to tell him that wasn't the only way.

We can get sucked into this trap. We can hang on to our too-heavy load too long because we have invested everything into our identity as carers. If we share the load – with paid carers who come in to help, or with a residential care home – then it's no more 'I, only I' but a new shared role where we have to give up a lot of our power and control. Not easy.

Not easy, but necessary. It only hurts us more to cling on to 'I, only I' when it's past time to let go and share the load.

Prayer

Heavenly Father, guard us from burn-out. Gently point out to us when we need to accept help, and when it is time to let others take over. Give us compassion for ourselves as well as our loved one.

Self-care suggestion

Do something just for you – something that will not benefit anyone else in any way. Allow at least ten minutes for total selfishness today!

3

But they're my responsibility

Honour your father and your mother, so that you may live long in the land the LORD your God is giving you. (Exodus 20.12)

Each one of you also must love his wife as he loves himself, and the wife must respect her husband. (Ephesians 5.33)

Whoever welcomes one of these little children in my name welcomes me; and whoever welcomes me does not welcome me but the one who sent me. (Mark 9.37)

When we're struggling with the big decision, it's very easy to find scriptural passages that we can beat ourselves up with. But that's a misuse of God's Word. As Christians, we are indeed called to obey God's laws and outstrip the Pharisees of old in our righteousness, but when Jesus interpreted those laws to us he insisted that love be our touchstone and benchmark, and asked of us much more than a surface apparent obedience. It's what's going on inside us – our motives, our heart – that matters.

The decision to move loved ones from their home/our home into a residential care facility is a painful one but we need to take a close, keen look at why we are considering it. Is it to rid us of an inconvenience, a burden on our time and energy? To make life easier for us so we can get out and enjoy ourselves? In other words, for selfish reasons? Or is our real love for them at the heart of the decision? Will they be better cared for by trained people, in a specially adapted environment, with much more on offer for stimulation, more company, a higher quality of care than we can manage, especially in our currently exhausted state?

We can't kid ourselves. We always know what our main motivation is – love or selfishness.

And real honesty demands that we admit that our motives get a bit mixed. There's always a bit of selfishness, no matter how loving we are. We are human, and self-preservation is a natural instinct. But we have a solution. We can take it to the Lord.

Prayer

Lord Jesus, I get myself all tangled up trying to get my head clear on this. I know I fail you and my loved one so often. Please pour your love into me and enable me to see what is best for __. Help me hang on to the truth so that, as I try to do the best for him/her, I can trust that you will be doing your best for both of us.

Self-care suggestion

Look at your hands: see the fingers, the knuckles, the skin on the back of your hands. Turn them over and see your palms – the lines that show the wear and tear of the years. Human hands. Hands you've used to care and to help and to do your best. Now think of God's hands – those amazing hands that created the universe, that were nailed to a cross. Imagine placing your hand in his. He'll hold you securely.

4

Join the club

Let's get this absolutely clear. The only carers – spouses, parents, sons or daughters – who do not feel guilt when they first seriously consider their loved one moving into residential care are few and far between. So far, I haven't met any.

So guilt comes with the territory. And it is a complete waste of energy. A smoke-screen that will prevent you from seeing clearly what is best for your loved one as well as for you.

But guilt's hard to get rid of. I haven't. It sits on my shoulder and whispers in my ear. Sometimes it points and shouts. But it rarely goes away.

Back in the 1970s a woman called Shirley Conran wrote a best-seller called *Superwoman*. It described in minute detail how to do everything – from decorating your own house to maintaining your car, arranging flowers, buying bed linen – and holding down a responsible job and having children too. This was the era of what the late Helen Gurley Brown named 'Having It All' (and wrote another book about).

It was a lie, and produced countless exhausted women beating themselves up because they discovered they couldn't do it all. And so guilt came to stay in the hearts and minds of every working woman who felt she wasn't making the grade.

Now many of that generation are finding themselves squashed in an impossible sandwich between the demands of their grandchildren (whose parents are both out working) and their own elderly parents, and/or an older partner.

The 'you can do it all' message continues until something has to give. The crunch will always be painful. Facing up to one's own limitations is hard. But necessary. Especially when the well-being of vulnerable youngsters or old people is at stake.

Yes, you think you should be able to do it all. You swallowed the lies just as I did. The truth is you can't. I can't. And the time will come when you will need help. When for the benefit of your loved one, you will need to hand over the day-to-day responsibilities to someone else.

As the manager of one care home said to me, 'The difference is that we get to go home at the end of our shift. You don't. And there are half a dozen of us. Only one of you.'

So don't feel guilty because you can't do it all. Even can't do any of it any more. You're completely fine as you are – simply normal. Not superwoman!

Prayer

Lord Jesus, it seems so difficult to admit our weakness and our limitations, yet you long for us to turn to you so that you can help us. Give us the honesty and wisdom to do just that!

Self-care suggestion

It isn't weakness to admit weakness. It's strength. Start today, being honest with yourself about what you can and can't do. You don't have to do it all!

5

Be prepared

<hr/>

At that time the kingdom of heaven will be like ten virgins who took their lamps and went out to meet the bridegroom.   (Matthew 25.1)

We often battle on too long, so a crisis erupts and our loved one suddenly needs to be admitted to residential care. When this happens, you will have little if any choice of which facility he or she will go to. Places are severely limited and it will be a case of where there is a room or a bed.

This is not a good outcome. Not a loving way to make the transition from home to residential care. The key is to be prepared in advance.

Now – when it's early days, even when it's too early – is the time to get a list of local residential homes that cater to your loved one's needs. For example, some homes will not accept dementia patients, others will. Some have two separate facilities on the same site, so that your loved one can be provided with appropriate care from familiar people as the condition progresses.

Next, go and visit, either with a friend or with your loved one, if it will not distress him. Managers understand that you need to see what the facilities are like. But be aware, they will be putting on a show – showing you the home at its best.

This need not be a problem. There are plenty of homes where the best is what the residents experience every day. We had a lovely meal when checking out one home – the one my husband is now in. And the food is still excellent every day!

Nowadays, in a savage market economy, we have all been turned into customers. And whether the local authority will be paying all, some, or none of the fees involved, your loved one is the customer – and you on her behalf – so the old motto prevails: *Caveat emptor*. Let the buyer beware!

It's good to pray for guidance before you set out. To go calmly and pay attention to everything you see and hear. Ask questions. Gather information – and impressions. Write it down, either then or as soon afterwards as you can. And pray over it: is this where you want him to be, Lord?

Take your time. Try to see every suitable home on your list. Meet the manager and the staff, and if possible talk to some of the residents.

Then you will be able to create a shortlist – and when the time comes, or a crisis erupts, you will be informed and better able to choose and deal with the transition.

Prayer

Guide us, Lord, as we look ahead on our loved one's behalf. Guide us to the right residential facility. Help us to know which is the right one, the best one for him/her. Give us discernment, and trust in you.

Self-care suggestion

Write things down. Gather brochures, print details off the internet, and add your own notes. You want to be able to remember your honest impressions: 'smelt nice and fresh', 'friendly staff', or 'smelt of urine', 'miserable, unfriendly manager'. Trust your own impressions.

6

Checking it out

———◆◆◆———

Ask and it will be given to you; seek and you will find; knock and the
door will be opened to you.   (Matthew 7.7)

When you're thinking about, or inspecting, residential care facilities,
it is a good idea to be clear about what you are looking for and why.

If you've got to the burn-out and total desperation stage, it can
seriously impair your judgement. That's a polite way of saying that
you'll be tempted to think, 'Anywhere will do! Just free me from this
unbearable burden!' That's perfectly legitimate. Just don't let it lead
to later regrets.

At the other end of the spectrum is the person who really does not
want to let go. If that's you, you'll be able to find plenty of objections
to even the best care home. Nowhere will be suitable. Because you
don't want it to be.

Wherever you are on this, you need some hard-won objectivity –
and unselfishness. Your loved one needs to be well looked after by
well-trained and competent staff. If they are pleasant, that's good. If
they are genuinely caring, that's great! The facilities need to be right.
What does your loved one need, and is it provided?

Working out in advance what matters will make your visit easier.
Nowadays, one would hope that standards would generally be quite
high – but the public sector has been cash-starved for a while and
the private sector is expected to make profits, so personally checking
out the home before your loved one is admitted is essential. A well-
run home will welcome your visit and the staff will be happy to
answer your questions.

I found our inspection visits worked well as 'days out'. The comfortable, welcoming home that gave us an excellent meal won extra
brownie points with my husband. Being introduced to – and left
with – one of the residents who told us how happy she was there

made a good impression too. It's not surprising that that is where he's now happily settled.

If you can find a residential home that you'd be happy spending your last days in, then you've probably found a good one for your loved one. If you'd have to be dragged there kicking and screaming, then don't touch it with a bargepole!

You need to know that you've chosen the best care available. Then you will have a measure of peace about the move.

Prayer

Give us wisdom, Lord Jesus, and guide us to the right place.

Self-care suggestion

Give yourself time. Try to be well rested and open-minded. If you don't like a place, that's OK. Keep looking until you find the right place. There is one out there!

7

Knowledge is power

Teach me knowledge and good judgment.   (Psalm 119.66)

Most private residential homes produce glossy brochures with attractive photographs and glowing descriptions of the care they aim to provide. It looks so perfect. But of course it's meant to. Homes in the commercial sector are businesses, run as businesses, and you or your loved one is the customer – the customer they want to like the product or the promises enough to want to buy.

It is a big commitment. You don't know how long your parent/spouse/child will be resident in the home, so it is important that the choice is a good one. Moving from one's own familiar home into residential care can be very upsetting, especially if it is not entirely voluntary or under the person's full control. Making another move to a second care home because the first did not work out will be even more difficult.

Good preparation – finding out which care homes are appropriate and provide the right level of care, checking them out personally, asking questions and getting answers – will ease the way. And everything you can do to ease the way will help you as well as your loved one.

It's important that you should feel comfortable – with the staff, the home and its routines – so that you can provide the support that your loved one needs. If you're not comfortable, you won't be so happy about visiting, popping in, spending time there.

So familiarization is necessary. You need to know the names of the staff you'll be dealing with and what their job titles mean. This does vary, as each home tends to decide on its own titles. If you don't know, don't be afraid to ask. It will make dealing with them and any problems down the line much easier.

Discuss with the manager or senior carer how you can best support your loved one. This can range from taking them out on a regular basis to specialist laundry, personal care such as manicures, joining in activities and outings, joining them for meals. You will feel much more confident and welcome knowing what you can do.

It's also helpful to know what they would prefer you not to do – for example, about bringing in food and drink. Sometimes this is allowed and sometimes not, so checking before you do it is a good idea.

You may feel overwhelmed by all the information you gather before the move, but rest assured: it will smooth the way.

Prayer

Lord Jesus, it feels such a huge step into scary foreign territory. Please be with us as we start on this stage of the journey and give us wisdom and good judgement.

Self-care suggestion

Be gentle with yourself. There's a lot to think about and your emotions may leap up and thump you when you least expect it. Try to build in time to reflect and to relax.

8

Baby steps

———•◆•———

Come with me by yourselves to a quiet place and get some rest.

(Mark 6.31)

It feels a huge thing to do, moving your loved one into residential care. And it can be. Especially when you're stricken with guilt as well as exhaustion to the point of burn-out. And worse, if she does not want to go.

Elderly parents can cling to their homes past the point where they are safe to remain there. Previously unhappy relationships do a flip-flop in the mind of the parent or estranged spouse and suddenly you're the only person in the world who can look after them.

You feel that you're going to have to prise her fingers off the front gate and carry her kicking and screaming to the car, shaming you all the way down the street.

There is a way. A kind way, for both of you. It's called respite. If you haven't yet taken advantage of this facility, then you have a lovely surprise awaiting you!

Most residential care facilities offer respite care, where you can book your loved one in for a weekend, a week, or longer. It is much easier to explain that you need a weekend to get well enough to continue caring, or go somewhere, do something you really need to do. Having sussed out the local residential homes, you will know which one offers this facility and will suit best.

It's crucial to assure your loved one that you're not going to dump them there! That this genuinely is a short break – a little holiday for you both. And it is much easier to pacify your guilt and strengthen your own backbone to go through with it . . . when it's just for a weekend.

This is how we began. I had got to burn-out. We had looked at a couple of homes and discovered a lovely one. When we were being

16

shown round, the manager said, 'This room is empty because it's the one we use for respite breaks.'

I could hear the bell ring loud and clear. 'It's available at the moment?' I asked.

'Yes,' she replied.

We continued our tour but I knew we had found the right place. My husband was willing to co-operate and enjoyed his weekend. I managed to recover enough to carry on for a few more months. Then he returned to the care home for another weekend, and gradually the periods at home decreased and the periods in the care home increased. He is now settled very contentedly there full-time.

You may find this works for you.

Prayer

Lord Jesus, you know what is right for us to do. Guide us and smooth the way ahead.

Self-care suggestion

What would you do with some time off, some time just for you? Is there somewhere you'd like to go? Take a little time to think how you would really use a respite break to get the most out of it. A plan for something really enjoyable will stiffen your spine when the time comes so you don't back out!

9

Arm's length

———•═•———

For what do they care about the families they leave behind?

(Job 21.21)

My friend used to drive two hours each way to check on her widowed father, almost blind, pretty shaky but determined to continue living in his own home. The cost to her was not simply in time and petrol but in stress and worry, waiting for that telephone call . . .

Another friend is the length of the country away from her elderly mother. Fortunately there is an airport near her home and she has made good use of it over the past few years. Again, it is costly in time and money, and stress and worry.

The days of the close-knit family living on the same street, in the same town or village, are long gone. For some that's a good thing, but as parents and relatives become elderly and in need of care, and our lives become increasingly busy and committed, it's one more anxiety when we live far away from them. One more source of guilt.

There's now even a name for us: the sandwich generation. The folk squashed in the middle of the sandwich, between elderly parents/relatives needing help and attention, and children and grandchildren who also need help and attention.

You can get squashed very thinly indeed. And then be no use to anybody.

There's no point saying that you must prioritize – because who can prioritize love? They each belong at the top of the heap! So you end up juggling, which is the best you can do. And getting exhausted, and feeling guilty, or cross that they won't move nearer, or into a care home where you'll know they're being well looked after.

It's a tightrope, knowing when to nudge gently, offer information about care homes, suggest visits to inspect or to visit friends happily settled in one – and when to back off, leave it alone, bite your tongue.

And it's really difficult knowing just when to leap in the car or on that plane and charge to the rescue – and when not to. When to leave it to the social workers and mental health professionals.

In the end, all you can do is the best you can do. And I'm sure you're doing that already.

Prayer

We do care, Lord Jesus, but it's hard – we live so far away, we have our own problems ... and we feel guilty that we can't do more to help. Show us what you want us to do in this situation.

Self-care suggestion

If you're a worrier, you'll be finding this situation very difficult, but there does come a time when you need to trust the people on the ground. Caring for yourself in this situation may involve a goodly amount of self-talk about trust and letting go!

10

Time to blow the whistle

Defend the weak and the fatherless; uphold the cause of the poor and the oppressed. Rescue the weak and the needy; deliver them from the hand of the wicked. (Psalm 82.3–4)

How long can this go on? This is a question we often ask ourselves, whether we are the sole carer or a family member or friend of someone who needs care. Sometimes the question is raised because of our increasing age, poor health, ability to continue. Sometimes it is because the person we are caring for – or caring about – is deteriorating and needs increasing levels of care.

Independence is something we admire, but it can be counterproductive when someone who needs help adamantly refuses it. Knowing when to draw the line is difficult. Social workers and mental health staff may believe the good face our friend/parent/spouse is able to present for the brief period of their visit.

Maintaining the dignity of the person involved, respecting his wishes, is crucial. But if we are convinced that he is not coping, that the quality of his life is significantly damaged by his situation, and especially if his safety is threatened, then it is time to bring our concerns to the relevant people.

Careful observation, taking notes of what happens and what you see and hear, will give you objective evidence, which needs to be presented as calmly as possible. You are not being a nuisance and the social workers and mental health workers have a duty of care for the person involved. You may have information they don't and they should listen respectfully to you.

If at all possible, have someone with you during the conversation. Voice your concerns. And if you lose your cool, don't worry. We all do! You're justifiably worried and trying to get your point across.

And if you don't succeed the first time, keep taking notes and keep asking. In this climate of financial cuts, sadly it's often the squeaky hinge that gets the oil.

Prayer

Give us courage and wisdom to do what is best, Lord Jesus. If we need to stand up to an uncaring authority, give us calm and the right words. You who championed the poor and weak, strengthen and enable us.

Self-care suggestion

If you can share your burden of worry with other family members, now is the time to do so. It can help to have someone else's perspective, but don't bite their heads off if they don't always agree with you! This is a difficult situation for everyone concerned.

11

When disaster strikes

Whatever disaster or disease may come, and when a prayer or plea
is made by anyone among your people . . . then hear from heaven, your
dwelling-place.   (2 Chronicles 6.28–30a)

Maybe you were aware that time was running out. Everything had
been going well, even surprisingly well, for a while. But you knew
there would come a crunch time.

It appears to be quite common for an accident or sudden bout of
ill health to precipitate entry to residential care. And sometimes it
comes as a huge relief to relatives who have been suggesting, even
arguing the case for, residential care for a while.

I have a very independent friend who needed a hip replacement
operation but afterwards found herself quite unable to cope alone.
She fought it for a while, until her concerned friends blew the
whistle. Now she is happily settled in an excellent care facility in her
home town, still among friends.

The sudden hospitalization, or even death, of a person who has been
the sole carer for a partner with dementia or other high-dependency
condition may be the trigger for the partner to move to residential
care.

And despite the upset involved, there is blessing too. Crisis removes
guilt. What has to be done for the well-being of the people involved
takes clear precedence over feelings, and the move can be achieved
swiftly.

It's always better to be prepared. To have checked out what's available and how it will be paid for. If you've been avoiding this, know
that crises do happen and then events will take over. You may feel
guilty about checking out care homes without telling your parent/
spouse, but in the long run, it is the more caring thing to do. After
all, you may never need it.

Prayer

Be with us, Lord Jesus. Keep us close to you and reassure us that you are in charge, whatever happens.

Self-care suggestion

The British panacea for any crisis situation is hot sweet tea. Have some, and make sure you've got a box of tissues to mop up the tears.

12

I give up

But a Samaritan . . . took pity on him. He . . . bandaged his wounds. . . .
Then he put the man on his own donkey, brought him to an inn and took
care of him. The next day he took out two denarii and gave them to the
innkeeper. 'Look after him,' he said, 'and when I return, I will reimburse
you for any extra expense you may have.'   (Luke 10.33–35)

For most of us, there comes a time when we cannot look after our
loved ones appropriately or safely on our own at home. For some of
us, our own health breaks down and help is crucial. Bringing in
a paid carer or having our loved one go into residential care can be
very painful. It feels like disloyalty. Admitting defeat. Failure. There's
guilt and lots of other negative feelings. But if you've got to the stage
where you're simply saying to yourself or a friend, 'I just can't do this
any more', and you know it's the truth, then it is time for a change
in the way your loved one is cared for.

Having you struggling on when you're way past the end of your
strength is no way to provide good care. It's a hard choice, but for
the best if your loved one will receive better-quality care from someone else.

You're not giving up – you're delegating. Like the Good Samaritan,
your love and care continues but in a different way. Notice how he
didn't stay on for as long as the injured man needed him. He did the
initial bit, then he paid for continued help, which he planned and
supervised.

This now becomes your role, and it is just as important, just as
caring.

Prayer

Dear Lord, help me to know when it is right to bring in other carers
or make the move to residential care. Guide us to the best people,

the best place for my loved one. Go ahead of us and smooth the way to make the transition as easy as possible. And comfort me, Lord, as I let go.

Self-care suggestion

You may find yourself moping and not knowing what to do with your new free time. Be gentle with yourself: you're doing a kind of grieving as you let go and deal with the change in your relationship. Then use some of the new time to get real rest. Don't tackle long ignored chores! Rest, nap and sleep as a priority. Treat yourself rather like a convalescent until you start to feel more like yourself again. It takes time, but it will happen.

13

Changing roles

From [Christ] the whole body, joined and held together by every supporting ligament, grows and builds itself up in love, as each part does its work. (Ephesians 4.16)

'You've got your life back.' So my well-meaning friends said when they heard that my husband was now settled into a residential care facility. Wrong.

True, you are no longer the hands-on carer. But if you were your loved one's primary carer, spouse, only son or daughter, then the buck still stops with you. Your responsibility for their care and well-being continues. It's only your role that has changed.

And in many ways, it is *more* difficult at arm's length. Because you cannot know everything that is going on. And that can produce more stress, not less!

This is going to be a settling-in period for you too, as you get to know the home, the staff, the routines, and as your relationship with your loved one changes, as you delegate her care to others.

But there is plenty left for you to do. And it is important for your loved one. Your continuing responsibilities include advocacy. For example, in the later stages of dementia, she may lose the power of speech. And even in earlier stages, you may need to speak for her so that her needs are attended to.

Your relationship with your loved one strengthens his self-esteem. Being quite a bit younger than my husband, I reckon I'm currently playing the trophy wife, so I try to dress nicely when I visit – and I'm definitely donning the glad rags for the Christmas party!

Your shared life with your loved one provides reinforcement of who he was as a person before the illness or disability struck, and you can draw on this to bolster his individuality. How you treat him – and ensure the staff treat him – will ensure that his dignity is maintained.

Your companionship is valuable in itself, as is the fact that you are the link with other members of the family and the community at large, preventing your loved one from feeling isolated.

You have a new and important role. You haven't been made redundant!

Prayer

You know how we feel, Lord. Comfort our hurt and loneliness. Give us new resources for the tasks ahead. And give us hope and joy.

Self-care suggestion

You may feel a bit lost at first, without the person you have focused on for so long. Treat yourself gently and kindly, as if you were getting over flu. Give yourself time, feed yourself well and healthily, and you will – I promise you! – come through this too, and be able to cope well with the situation.

14

Time to let go

There is a time . . . a time to embrace and a time to refrain.

(Ecclesiastes 3.1, 5b)

It was probably guilt that had me running backwards and forwards from our house to the residential home. If he'd lost something, needed anything, I'd drop everything and rush down there to sort it out.

Finally, the manager took me aside and said very kindly, 'One day, you're going to have to let go.'

I was shocked. Let go? But we're married!

It has taken time, but gradually I have come to trust the staff, trust that my husband is being well looked after – better than I could do. That this is the right place, the right care provision for him at this stage. And I have surrendered my burden. Let go.

It hasn't been easy. For a while I floundered. Who am I now? I was a wife, lover, friend, housekeeper, cook, then carer, mother-substitute . . . Now I am someone who goes over for coffee and takes him out on Fridays. Friend? Girlfriend? The power of attorney gives me full responsibility for things such as the finances – so I'm also company secretary, chief executive of the business that is my husband, on his behalf.

Whether your loved one in residential care is a child or spouse or parent, your role changes. Who are you now? And can you accept it?

There is a time to let go. Resistance makes it harder, for both of you.

Prayer

When I look to you, Lord God, I know who I am. I am your beloved child. The apple of your eye. My name is written on the palm of your hand. If you had a wallet, my photograph would be in it. If you had a fridge, my picture would be on the front. This is who we really are – beloved by you, special to you. And that never changes.

Self-care suggestion

Sometimes the things we turn to for comfort are not good for us. I spent a chunk of last year comfort eating – and putting on weight, not to mention raising my cholesterol! We need safe, healthy things, and people, to turn to when we are in need of comfort. And it is our responsibility to find them. Yes, one more burden! But it is well worth it. Maybe start off with making a list . . .

15

Finding your peace

————•◦•————

If it is possible, as far as it depends on you, live at peace with everyone.

(Romans 12.18)

Not all residents of care homes are loved ones. Old age, dementia and dependency do not suddenly transform people into loving dads/mothers or husbands/wives. And instead of a reservoir of mutual love and happy memories, there can be a quagmire of unhappy memories, of abuse and even violence.

But the honourable spouse is left with the marriage vow's requirement to hang in there in sickness as in health, and the honourable parent or child is held by their sense of responsibility – whatever the person may have done to them in the past.

It is possible – as in the case of a friend of mine and her previously abusive mother – that the final years bring an unexpected bounty of forgiveness and compassion, even love, so that old scores are left behind and unhappy memories are overtaken by a new tenderness.

Each one of us is in a different, unique place. Our loved one may be an angel, an obvious monster, or a devil in disguise who has a smiling face for everyone but us. Whatever our situation, if there has been abuse in the past, we need to protect ourselves from further harm. And we need to be honest with ourselves about what we can do as far as visiting and outings and other involvement are concerned.

Your decisions may be different from mine but need to be made. Reaching a settlement with ourselves that we are comfortable with will enable us to do what we can with good grace and a peaceful heart.

Prayer

Dear Lord Jesus, you promised us your peace. Help us to recognize what we can do and what we cannot do, and give us peace about what we choose to do.

Self-care suggestion

Don't feel guilty if your loved one going into care is an enormous relief. Instead, be grateful and think about what you can do now that you couldn't do before. Then choose one thing and do it!

16

Down with guilt!

Therefore, there is now no condemnation for those who are in Christ
Jesus. (Romans 8.1)

When the person you've been caring for goes into a residential
facility, people often say things like, 'You can get on with your life
now.' They think that you've acquired a kind of freedom. But you
haven't. Just because you don't share a home, a table, or a bed any
more does not sever the relationship. In fact, even when one party
no longer recognizes the other and the relationship has become
completely one-sided, it still remains.

But there is a change. Distance does not necessarily make the heart
grow fonder. It often simply makes you worry more – because you
no longer have the moment-to-moment information about how your
loved one is doing. And visiting time can be extra painful because of
the jolts as unexpected changes take you by surprise.

And when you're on your own, as well as the beastly loneliness,
there's the ever-ready-to-pounce guilt. Folk who don't understand
why your loved one is in residential care, who only saw her for half
an hour and on a good day at that, may express their disapproval
and suggest that what you've done is 'dumped her'.

Read my lips: you haven't. And you haven't stopped caring for her
either. A friend of mine who has a lot of experience in the care world
says that it's the people who really care for their loved ones who place
them in residential care – because they want the best for them.

When you've done the absolute best that you can do, there is no
reason to feel guilt. But we often fall into the perfectionist trap where
even our best is not good enough! But it is all that we can do. So:
down with guilt!

Prayer

Lead us from darkness, Lord Jesus, and into your light. Take away our guilt and self-recrimination. Stop us from beating ourselves up and give us instead your reassurance that we are loved and accepted by you. Give us your peace.

Self-care suggestion

Try practising today's key phrases: 'I'm doing my best'; 'Down with guilt!' Write them down if you need to. Put them on sticky notes and place them on the mirror. Keep reminding yourself – because it's true!

17

Talk to me!

---·◆·---

The tongue is a small part of the body . . . but no human being can
tame the tongue.   (James 3.5a, 8a)

When it was just the two of you, you did everything. Now, that caring
is being done by other people, and there is a temptation to think that
they won't do it as well as you. That they won't understand your
loved one or his needs as well as you.

And sometimes you'll be right. Often, though, you'll be wrong,
and you're conjuring up mountains out of molehills quite simply
because you don't have enough information. You're not there 24/7.

When you feel that there is a problem and you try to talk to a staff
member about a concern, sometimes they seem too busy or un-
willing to give you the attention you feel it deserves.

Or maybe you haven't plucked up the courage to mention it.
You're worried that to voice anything that sounds like criticism could
be seen as interference, or might impact negatively on your loved
one's experience.

It's not easy to get this right. Care home staff can be sensitive
to what they may take to be a slur on the standard of their care.
And you may, especially at the beginning, lack the experience or the
courage to say what you feel needs to be said – until it builds up and
comes rushing out, not at all in the calm and reasonable way you
had planned it!

You should be involved. You should be kept informed. But keeping
residents' families happy comes quite a way down the list of pressing
day-to-day matters for care home staff. And that's understandable.
You want them to focus on providing attention and kindly care to
your loved one.

The job of creating good communication and maintaining an easy
relationship with the home is one more important task for you. As

you become increasingly familiar with the home and the people there, you'll find that your confidence builds. You will also know who the best staff member to talk to is. And how to tackle things.

It takes time. You'll make mistakes. (I did! Still do. When I'm worried I have a tendency to rush in headlong . . .) But you'll find that care home staff and managers are remarkably forgiving. They've been round the block before. They know where you're coming from and they understand.

Prayer

Guard our tongues and guard our hearts, Lord God, that we may build good relationships with the care home staff.

Self-care suggestion

If you get upset when talking to staff, or maybe get a bit impatient or cross, don't beat yourself up about it afterwards. It's so easy for our emotions to take over. This is where you need to learn to forgive yourself, then think through how you can do better next time. Because there will be a next time.

18

How much is enough?

———◆◆◆———

I hope to visit you and talk with you face to face, so that our joy may be complete. (2 John 1.12b)

In the very early days, when your loved one is settling in to life in residential care, you have a major challenge: how much visiting should you do?

If she was admitted because you were burnt-out or too ill to keep on looking after her, then you're going to need to take some time out to recover. But how do you reassure your loved one that she hasn't been dumped?

On the other hand, you may miss him so much – or feel so guilty – that you want to spend as much time as possible with him. It's been known for wives to turn up to help with breakfast and then stay for the rest of the day.

Typically, spouses tend to stay very involved, while sons and daughters are able to let go a little more easily. If you want to continue to be involved with your loved one's care, it's a good idea to ask what would be helpful. You might be surprised at the welcome you receive!

The pattern of visiting will evolve just as your loved one's condition does, but it's wise to establish a pattern – for your own sake and, if your loved one is able to recognize it, for her reassurance too. And it needs to be a pattern that does not become a rod for your own back.

In the early stages, you may be advised to give your loved one a certain amount of time *without* visiting, to give him a chance to settle, make his own friends and patterns – if he is able. Over-frequent visiting can convey your anxiety and lack of trust, to the staff and also to your loved one, and unsettle him, rather than help him settle.

You need to take into consideration both the commitments in your own life and how the home operates. The home where my husband is offers an excellent programme of in-house activities and outings, which he enjoys. Our Friday outings seem sufficient for him at present, but that may change.

It's your decision. And if it doesn't work for you, you can change it.

Prayer

You know that we want to do our best, Lord God, but this is new territory and we need help. Please guide us towards a healthy and loving solution for us and our loved one.

Self-care suggestion

You need to monitor how it feels. You're aiming for enough visits to keep your loved one – and you – happy. You don't have to stick to the first routine you try. You can experiment until you find what works. And while you do, be kind to yourself. This isn't easy.

19

All about clothes

———•◦•———

And why do you worry about clothes?   (Matthew 6.28)

At first, delegating your loved one's laundry is a great blessing and a genuine weight off your shoulders. It comes at a price, of course: the necessity of labelling clothes.

When I first put labels in my husband's clothes, I found it very sad. It seemed to underline the fact that such personal things, which had once been my domain, would be so no longer.

I originally used iron-on labels. I suppose I had no idea how long they would be necessary – or what kind of laundering they would be getting. Soon, I needed to change to sew-on labels. I've now got in the habit of bringing the roll of labels, needle and white cotton two or three times a year and doing a wardrobe overhaul.

The first time I did that, I discovered some unlabelled trousers in the wardrobe that definitely did not belong to my husband. And he seemed to be rather low on supplies of handkerchiefs and pyjamas. This was easily solved, simply by bringing it to the attention of the staff. It's generally accepted that laundry staff do their best, but even in the best-run home clothes go AWOL. I've heard this attributed to the clothes-eating monster – probably to be found in any residential institution!

Next, clothes came back from the laundry with tears in one sleeve. We still haven't worked out how that was happening. But it's clear that it's up to me to keep an eye on my husband's clothes. He would happily wear the same stained sweater, shirt or trousers every day. I have, in extremis, taken home particularly unpleasant trousers and given them a thorough soak and wash.

Once again, this is an area that is dependent on good relations and communications with the staff. You don't want to be a nuisance, but you do want your loved one dressed each day in her own clothes and as clean and fresh as is reasonable, bearing in mind her problems. This isn't an area for perfectionism. A stained top doesn't matter compared with a happy visit together.

Prayer

Give us generosity of spirit and understanding – of the problems of our loved ones and of the other residents, but also the problems faced by the staff who do their best for them. May we deal with any matters of concern with gentleness.

Self-care suggestion

This is a tricky but very familiar problem area. I've got a notebook in which I've listed all my husband's clothes, so I can monitor whether he has everything he should have. I do it unobtrusively so as not to offend anyone. It might be worth a try if you're concerned.

20

Trouble at mill

———◦•◦———

Blessed are those who have regard for the weak.   (Psalm 41.1a)

There was a new resident on my husband's corridor. She became upset when she was left on her own and cried out. This was distressing to the other residents and my husband told me about it. Several times.

So I mentioned it to the manager. But I got the feeling that this was one of those no-win situations for her; she'd been told about it so many times by residents and their families already today that it was quite understandably beginning to annoy her.

I'm quite sure that the manager was doing her best to sort this out, but what do you do when you're *not* confident that your concerns are being listened to?

I recently spent an afternoon learning about safeguarding vulnerable adults (the Methodist Church training module, Safer Space). The programme offers a useful procedure for when one has concerns:

1 Observe
2 Record
3 Respond
4 Refer

Paying attention and writing down one's observations is a good start. You need to know who to take your concerns to – and who then to refer it to if you're not satisfied. Most residential facilities have a complaints procedure. We all hope that we will never need to use it, but it is wise to know what to do, just in case.

Prayer
Seeing on television care homes where residents have been ill treated is worrying, Lord. We ask you to protect the vulnerable and make us alert to signs of abuse.

Self-care suggestion

This is a delicate area. If you think that your loved one is being mistreated you're going to need extra support. Choose who you speak to with care, but do speak up.

21

Dealing with the hassles

For thou art with me; thy rod and thy staff they comfort me.

(Psalm 23.4b, AV)

Being on the outside is difficult, especially when your informant may not be 100 per cent reliable. This is something I trip over, and come home feeling, 'I really did not do that well'.

I tend to go rushing to the rescue, only to discover (so often) that things were not as I had been told. Or, shall we say, that there were two very different stories with little point of contact. So I need to extricate myself *and* everyone else involved, and try to save faces and preserve dignity all round.

After which I want to find a wall and bang my head against it!

In the enclosed space of a residential facility, misunderstandings happen, communications get mixed up and sometimes things go wrong. Rushing in where angels fear to tread only gets me entangled and drained.

Later, when the adrenalin has ebbed and peace has returned, I'll be able to write it off as just another of the inevitable hassles that seem to go with the territory. And there will be more. And we'll deal with them. Maybe with a little more wisdom this time!

Prayer

I really don't cope well with the tangles and the hassles – but you can, and you enable me, Lord. I may not come out of today with an A* but just maybe I did better than a D-minus!

Self-care suggestion

This is where you need to press the 'pause' button on your life! Sit down. Get yourself a nice cool drink, or cup of tea, and sip it slowly. Let the adrenalin ebb away and your blood pressure normalize. Take time out.

22

I want to go home

My people will live in peaceful dwelling-places, in secure homes, in undisturbed places of rest. (Isaiah 32.18)

Probably the hardest thing to deal with is when your loved one asks, 'When can I go home?' Or even worse, says, 'I want to come home!'

My husband used to have phases of this. I'd call them campaigns, where he would tell me how much better things would be at home. Which alerted me to the fact that there was some problem where he was.

In spring last year, someone mistakenly talked to him about the annual fee increase. Because of his memory problems, his sense of money and the value of money is not always in the twenty-first century, so when he discovered how much his room was costing, he was horrified. And a mega-campaign began because, of course, if he came home, everything would be free – bed, board, care – since that's how it is at home. Your mum and dad don't charge you money . . .

When you've already got a bellyful of guilt about your loved one being in a residential home, her plea – or demand – to come home, or return to her own home, twists your gut still further.

You can understand perfectly. If you were in your loved one's place . . . And that's where you have to step back. Chill, as the young would say. Because you're not in her place. She is in residential care because she needs to be. Because being at home did not work. Wasn't safe. Didn't offer the care she requires.

How you handle it depends on your loved one's condition. My husband's memory is so poor that I know now that if I don't get emotional, and don't make a big thing of explaining, producing counter-arguments and so on, we can ride over the hump comparatively smoothly. Then later I can find out why he is disturbed.

I have learned that blocking the wish to go home head on guarantees disaster. You'll get upset. They'll get upset.

You'll discover new skills as you tackle each of the hurdles you encounter. Your loved one will settle in and accept his new home. Some folk even gain a new lease of life, like my friend's mother-in-law, who after years of complaining and vowing that she would 'never go into a home', enjoys her new environment and friends enormously. A good residential care facility will improve the quality of your loved one's life. It may be hard to accept, but it is something good that you can offer him now.

Prayer

Keep us calm, Lord, when we feel the rug being pulled out from under our feet. When we feel threatened or faced with a situation that we feel we can't handle, remind us that you can handle this and all we need to do is trust you.

Self-care suggestion

If you got it wrong and made the situation worse, forgive yourself. It's a steep learning curve! If, under the pressure, you caved in and agreed that he or she could go to their own home, or come home to live with you, relax. If your loved one has dementia, the conversation is likely to have been forgotten about by the time you next visit . . . as long as *you* don't mention it. The key is for *you* to get calm first; then you can deal with this.

23

In this together

And our hope for you is firm, because we know that just as you share in our sufferings, so also you share in our comfort.

(2 Corinthians 1.7)

They're everywhere: folk with loved ones, especially parents, spouses, older brothers and sisters, in residential care. And a large percentage of loved ones suffer from dementia of one form or another.

It's like a 1960s spy film. Mention the password – dementia or care home – and the other party nods and launches into their story. This happens in shops, with the staff as well as other customers joining in. It happens in cafés, at the doctor's surgery and the dentist's, the hairdresser's and in the post office queue. Today the nice lady supervising a routine health check was telling me about her mother . . .

There's a lot of it about. But you don't find out until you start the ball rolling. It's still a very private thing, despite being nearly everyone's experience.

And that's a pity, because we're all amateurs, all beginners in this. The professionals don't really share their expertise. We're the ones with the real nitty-gritty knowledge and it would be great if we would all be more upfront and share!

I've been wondering if we need a ribbon to wear, to flag up to others in the know or in the same situation. Then maybe we'd have more conversations, learn some hard-earned tips.

The tip for me today was about staff at care homes. Don't get bothered or distressed because the staff member you spoke to doesn't seem well informed or bothered. They can't all be familiar with every resident. But there will be at least one who has made a close connection with your loved one. This is the person you need to seek out and keep in touch with. She or he will then be your main contact, who will keep you informed and reassure you.

I found this enormously comforting, to be reminded of the special someone at the care home where my husband lives who has made that contact with both of us. I'm very grateful for her and to her.

Prayer

We know we're not alone, holy Lord. You care for us and you have promised to be with us, closer than breathing, if we will only turn to you. Help us to turn to you and keep turning to you!

Self-care suggestion

It takes courage to start these conversations, and sometimes you'll meet blank faces and zero empathy. But more often than not you'll find yourself talking to someone in the same boat who is relieved to be able to talk to someone about it. You may find a new friend!

24

New faces

A new command I give you: love one another.　　　　John 13.34

Just when you've got your loved one settled, and you've built up good relationships with the staff (well, at least you know their names and can recognize them when you visit), inevitably there will be staff changes. Including at management level.

This can have a major impact on the home, the staff and the residents. I reckon that care staff and managers of care homes are a very special breed – pearls without price, and just as hard to find. As a result, sometimes that perfect person is not available, and someone takes over who is – shall we say – not quite so gifted.

Managerial styles seem to be on a continuum ranging from relaxed, homely, almost anything goes, to strictly by the rules, stay in your rooms and do as you're told. Drawing on our experience of a number of homes, we've met both extremes. We've even encountered staff rebellions, and resident rebellions. (My husband suggested, in the early days, that he write a soap series set in a care home – he reckoned it could be fertile ground for an entertaining comedy!)

A change of manager or staff means that you have to start all over again building a good relationship with them. They need to get to know you and that they can rely on you to play your part; you need to get to know them and trust them to do their job.

Your new role places new responsibilities on you, and building relationships with all these different people is crucial for your loved one's comfort and well-being.

Prayer
Top up my love and friendliness tanks, Lord, so that I can fuel those necessary relationships with the care home staff.

Self-care suggestion

You can't like everyone, so don't worry if you don't hit it off with particular staff members. You can pray about it and try a bit harder, but don't be hard on yourself. Getting to know them a bit better will often dissolve any frost between you.

25

No more Lone Ranger

Do not forget to do good and to share with others, for with such sacrifices God is pleased. (Hebrews 13.16)

Friday is the day when I visit and take my husband out for the day. But I won't be doing that today. Some of his family have come on holiday for a week and today they are taking him out.

But it's strange. I'm feeling twitchy about this. I'm used to being the Lone Ranger: the only family member within reach to solve all the problems, oversee his care, make sure everything is all right – and provide happy outings on Fridays. The one-stop shop.

So many carers slip into the need-to-be-needed trap, where their identity and sense of value comes from their caring role, at the expense of everything else. Then, when their loved one goes into a care facility or dies, their world's sudden emptiness plunges them into depression or other ill-health.

Even the Lone Ranger had Tonto as a side-kick. Carers need side-kicks and support. You can't do it Lone Ranger style for very long. I know. I tried. And now that I've handed over to an excellent team at the care home, I need to make sure that I don't slip back into Lone Ranger ways, thinking that I'm the only one who really knows him, who understands his illness, who can see what's happening.

I need to share the care and the outings. No more Lone Ranger.

Prayer

Help me to welcome what other people can do to help. Help me share, Lord.

Self-care suggestion

Plan something nice for you to enjoy when someone else offers to visit for a change. Yes, you may feel uncomfortable or fret a bit, but you can overcome it and enjoy yourself!

26

Compassion fatigue

—◆·◆·◆—

> Come to me, all you who are weary and burdened, and I will give
> you rest. (Matthew 11.28)

Think of those nasty bits at the bottom of a cup of real coffee. The
bits that get between your teeth and stick to your tongue.

It's a poor ending to a good cup of coffee. But that's how I sometimes feel, even after a nice visit with my husband.

I've read up about this, and reckon it's the toxic mix of adrenalin
and cortisol that floods our systems. Because we're tense. Tongue-
bitingly and teeth-grindingly patient. Walking on eggshells to avert
upsets. And watchful, trying to see one step ahead to prevent any
falls, disasters, spills, aggression . . .

I do wonder whether people who have had children are better
at this than I am. Have they a fund of experience to draw on that
I don't have?

Maybe not, because we all seem to go home exhausted. And wondering why, when really we haven't done anything much!

The explanation, I've discovered, lies in compassion: what we feel
for our loved one in their situation. The 'com' means 'with'. But when
you add the rest of it – 'passion' – think Christ's passion. Suffering.
When we feel compassion, we are entering into someone else's suffering, sharing it with them, feeling it with them or for them.

So it's not surprising that we come home feeling exhausted. If we
are compassionate people, it goes with the territory.

Prayer

Lord Jesus, you know that we get weary and over-burdened. This
situation becomes more than we can cope with. Thank you that
we don't have to cope alone, that you really are here to shoulder our
burdens and help us. Thank you, Lord.

Self-care suggestion

If you're suffering compassion fatigue, try to build in recovery time after a visit or outing. Plan it in advance, because you won't have the energy to think about it when you come back!

27

Once more on the roller coaster

———◆●◆———

I have learned the secret of being content in any and every situation . . . I
can do all this through him who gives me strength.

(Philippians 4.12b, 13)

Today's changeable weather – sunshine then showers then more
sunshine – has mirrored our day together.

We set out as strangers, seeming not to communicate at all.
By the time we had had lunch, he was chatty, I was more relaxed
and it was all right. And this is par for the course – complete
unpredictability.

I start off the trip thinking, yes, it's right that he's in the care
home. He obviously needs more care than I could provide without
significant help (which he has always refused). Then, when we seem
to be chatting 'normally' I start to change my mind. Maybe he could
come home? Maybe I could try again? Maybe I could manage?

But I know I couldn't. I've tried so many times and it hasn't worked.
And so the guilt sets in again, gnawing into my cheerfulness.

Then he suddenly says, as we drive along a very familiar road near
home, that he can't remember where we are, or what comes next.
And I become aware of the deterioration in his memory. There are
holes where the rest of us have information, memories, stuff we take
for granted to get us through our lives. He simply doesn't have that
any longer.

And I see that life could be very scary for him. The enclosed environment of the care home gives him real security and the comfort of
knowing that the folk around him are there to look after him. He is
accepting of that, comfortable with it. Anything else would now be
unsettling, disruptive, potentially harmful for him.

So although I don't like living alone, any thoughts I might entertain
of having him at home again I have to admit are selfish. And it won't

do. He is better where he is. He is being looked after better. He is safe and content.

And I must try to be so too.

Prayer

I haven't learned the secret of being content in this situation yet, Lord Jesus. Please help me and give me your strength.

Self-care suggestion

When is the most difficult time for you? This needs tackling head on, rather than letting it defeat you! Think how you could fill that time in a happy, healthy way. Plan for it, provide for it, do it!

28

Need a refill?

Love one another, for love comes from God.   (1 John 4.7)

Living on our nerves is exhausting. Squashing our normal reactions, forcing calm and patience and pleasant responses to *that* question or *that* comment for the *n*th time, costs us. Dealing with upsets without getting upset. Calming down an agitated adult who has few inhibitions or any awareness of his own strength. The list goes on and the price to us is inevitable exhaustion.

So yes, recovery is necessary. And preferably sleep, uninterrupted and healing, so that we can face another day. We will recover, and we will face another day on this journey. It usually takes me 36 hours, and then I'm back on my even keel.

But the dementia that afflicts my husband, and so many people, and the other degenerative diseases that so many suffer from, will not go away after a nice nap. Each day is one step further down the road of a terrible journey.

I am very grateful that although my husband is aware of his mental deterioration he is peacefully accepting and unconcerned. A friend's mother is upset by it, though. Helping her find her key the other day, she confided in me, 'I hate this!'

We all do. Our challenge is to hang on to the love we have for our parents/spouses/friends who have been turned into sometimes frightening strangers by these diseases – and to love ourselves enough to continue being of loving use to them.

Prayer

Heavenly Father, you know how drained and exhausted we get. Please refill us with your love, that we may have enough for ourselves and for our loved ones who need us so much.

Self-care suggestion

One of my favourite ways of being kind to myself is a bubble bath. What do you find soothes and restores you?

29

Relax!

The Lord is my shepherd . . . he leads me beside quiet waters, he refreshes my soul. (Psalm 23.1a, 2b, 3a)

I'm visiting my sister for the first time in years and I'm sleeping late every morning. At home I usually wake around 6 a.m., but here it's more like 9 a.m. before I see the light of day! My sister says not to worry about it. I've obviously got a sleep debt and I should just give myself the chance to catch up. I just hadn't realized.

This has to be a carer thing – where our own needs have been pushed so far down the heap that they disappear from our consciousness as we drive ourselves on. Does this sound familiar?

Here, away from my own environment, I realize that I've been driving myself. Keeping myself busy, busy – because I feel guilty if I'm not.

Now I'm aware of how silly that is. It doesn't help me or my husband. It just wears me out sooner. Uses up the energy and the patience and the empathy and all the resources that rightly belong to him.

So today, I'm going to relax and enjoy my 'time off' – without trying to do anything more productive!

Prayer

Heavenly Father, you long for us to accept your peace and love. Today, help us to relax and rest in your loving care for us.

Self-care suggestion

When you have time off, make it really off duty, and enjoy it!

30

What's the name for it?

———◆•◆•◆———

The Sovereign LORD will wipe away the tears from all faces.

(Isaiah 25.8)

You'd think you would get used to it – the pattern of visits each week. You would expect to fall into a pleasant routine, with your life working again, but something weird happens. The timing may be routine but the visit never is. And it doesn't get any easier, especially the going home afterwards.

It took me a while to work out what was going on. The word is bereavement. Walking away is like walking away from a funeral. The live relationship that was is gone. And we are left to get on with our lives without them. So of course we mourn. Mourning is the true name of the sadness we feel as we go home alone.

I am, in effect, a widow six days of the week; I am suffering a virtual bereavement. The same is true of the grown child of a parent in residential care. But we are without the support that most widows and bereaved children receive from their families and friends. Our bereavement is invisible because our loved ones are still alive. Another way of looking at it, where a partner is involved, is as a kind of divorce – except a divorcee can go out and start a new life, dancing, going on holiday, meeting new friends. If we hold to our marriage vows – 'till death us do part' – then we can't.

Each time I leave the care home where my husband is living, there is a parting. And the pain I feel is the death of my hopes and dreams for a happy life together, shattered by his illness. This is where we need others in the same situation – others who really understand our existence, neither fish nor fowl. And help us support one another.

Prayer

You understand, Lord, and you promise to dry our tears. Help us to lean on you.

Self-care suggestion

Don't block the pain. Don't try to numb it. Because if you do, you'll find that you block or numb every emotion, and the terrible greyness of despair and depression will take over your life. Believe me, I've been there and it's hard to get out. So, let yourself feel the pain. Buy the boxes of tissues. Weep. But stay alive. Being emotionally alive includes pain and sorrow as well as joy. Leave the door open to joy.

31

False impressions

———◆◆◆———

We who are strong ought to bear with the failings of the weak and not
to please ourselves.   (Romans 15.1)

We were having our usual weekly outing and stopped in a local
shop. It was quite busy and among the customers were two women
I knew. One greeted us cheerfully while the other was absorbed in
her shopping.

'You remember X, don't you?' I carefully give him the name to
trigger his memory.

The woman beams and says loudly, as if to an imbecile, 'Yes, of
course he does, don't you? You see me around quite regularly.' He
smiles and answers yes of course.

Then she spots the other friend whom I haven't seen for a
long time. 'And there's Y,' she says. Y and I hug and catch up as
quickly as we can. Again he says he remembers her. Of course he
remembers her.

Shopping finished, we leave the shop and walk back to the car,
where he turns to me and asks, 'Who on earth were those people?'

I explain, but it's obvious that he really cannot place them. And
then I ask the stupid question: 'So why did you say you knew them?'

'They seemed to be people I would know,' he replies.

But it festers. Because those two women now clearly believe that
he recognized them, remembered them, knew them. Nothing much
the matter with him, then, so why is he in a home?

There is something about our situation that can make us ultra-
sensitive. And that something is our wholly unnecessary guilt. My
reaction was wholly unnecessary, but I couldn't have thought that at
the time!

Prayer

Lord Jesus, help us to ignore the little things that can upset us. Help us to push them away when they try to come back and bother us. Give us strength to trust in your love instead.

Self-care suggestion

You don't have to please all of the people all of the time – though it can be tempting. Learn to let things go. Life will be much more relaxing and less stressful for you. So some people don't understand? That's only to be expected. Don't let it get to you.

32

After the visit

———•◆•———

Dear friends, do not be surprised at the fiery ordeal that has come on you . . . , as though something strange were happening to you.

(1 Peter 4.12)

We know it's hard to do, sometimes very hard to do. You gird your loins, pray your prayers, fix that smile on your face and make yourself go through with it. The weekly visit.

Whether it's a good visit or a bad one, you drive yourself through it, keeping up the smiles, the cheerful chatter, the reassurance, and covering up when pain or stress or difficult behaviour threatens to strip away your 'coping' façade.

Then you come home, leaving your loved one there.

Sometimes it's a relief. Sometimes it's really hard. But the backlash always hits you. Sometimes it gets to you before you reach the car. Or as you're turning out of the gates. Whichever, it lurks in wait to ambush you after a good visit, or tip you over the top when it's been a bad one.

Because there's always a price to pay. A reaction. And you simply have to recognize it and wait it out. It goes with the territory. In this abnormal situation, this reaction of ours is normal.

Think of it like flu, but shorter! It can be short and sharp or lingery and draggy. Spotting it, being aware of it for what it is enables us to deal with it – and the next visit.

Prayer

We know that we can't do this on our own, Lord God. We need your strength to enable us to visit, and come home in one piece. Protect us before, during and after the visit. Bless us and our time together.

Self-care suggestion

Be prepared. Plan for the aftermath. Take yourself for a bracing walk in the fresh air. Meet an understanding friend for coffee. Don't just slump!

33

You in your small corner

Accept one another, then, just as Christ accepted you, in order to bring
praise to God.   (Romans 15.7)

It had been a perfectly amicable visit. We had coffee and he chatted.
I heard about the good food and excellent chef at the residential
facility where he now lives. About the gentleman with the distin-
guished military career. And the new person on his corridor. There
were stories of his childhood, his father, and his schooldays.

And then, as other people came into the room, it was plain that
my audience was over and it was time for me to go.

Once our lives intersected, overlapped. There were shared activities,
interests. Now he lives here, with these people. This is his world. And
I am outside.

I had tried to tell him bits of family news, but it was plain that
his world no longer encompasses anything other than the people he
sees on a daily basis, and he was only interested in that.

I suppose it's not surprising, especially with the progress of dementia,
that his world should shrink. For those of us on the outside, it's hard
to accept – but we must.

Prayer

Give us generosity of heart, Lord Jesus, to accept our loved one's
inevitable move away from us, emotionally and psychologically as
well as physically in this care home. Comfort us with your love and
presence. Compensate us for the love we are losing.

Self-care suggestion

When a major source of support and love is lost, we need to ensure that we're not left floundering. This is when your friends and other family members become so important. It's clear that people with good support networks cope better than those who are more solitary. Now is the time to build or strengthen that network.

34

Powerlessness

—•◆•—

Above all else, guard your heart, for everything you do flows from it.
(Proverbs 4.23)

It was one of those days. Maybe it was time for one of those days – we had had a run of good ones. Anyway, I had a plan. It's always better to have a plan. But today it went out of the window within moments.

'I thought we'd go to that nice garden centre for coffee and then have a look at the clothing outlet for a few more roll necks for you,' I said cheerfully. 'We'll see if they have any bargains.' He likes both roll necks and bargains.

'I don't need any more roll necks,' he said.

I had checked his wardrobe the week before. He seemed to be catching the elbow of his roll necks somewhere and tearing holes in them. It looked to me that he certainly did need a few more. However, we are told that we must respect his wishes – and I've learned not to precipitate 'difficult behaviour'.

So: 'OK, we won't go to the clothes place.'

Instead I took him to a nice café along the road for coffee (and found myself on automatic pilot, stuffing a completely unnecessary and unplanned scone into my face). We set out again, with me trying to conjure up a Plan B. But at once, we're at cross purposes again. Yes, one of those days.

In the café, there was a rack of current newspapers for customers to read. I was interested to see in one of them a report that it isn't stress that causes the most heart attacks but powerlessness: 'jobs which leave workers little freedom to make decisions sharply increase risk', according to a Europe-wide study reported in *The Lancet*.

Tell us about it!

Prayer

Guard my heart, Lord. This situation we are in makes me feel powerless and helpless. Remind me that you are in charge and that I can trust in you.

Self-care suggestion

Succumbing to heart disease is not going to help either us or our loved ones, so ensuring that we care for ourselves is essential. If you feel chest pain to do with stress, take slow, deep breaths and try to distract yourself so you don't panic and make it worse! Then get it checked out at the first opportunity.

35

Mrs Fix-it gives up

Who of you by worrying can add a single hour to your life? Since you cannot do this very little thing, why do you worry about the rest?

(Luke 12.25–26)

Are your shoulders, like mine, bent with the burden you are carrying? There is another way, and last week I decided to try it. Put my money where my mouth is, so to speak!

My friend had reminded me to pray before setting out for our outing – so this time I used the prayer to resign from being in charge, opting instead for God-in-charge, with me aiming for obedient trust. So off we went.

But when we got to our destination, I couldn't get a long-stay parking space. And then none of the places open for lunch appealed to him. What to do? I'd promised to do obedient trust, so instead of losing it (always the easier option!), I opened up the car and we headed out of town.

I suddenly thought of a nice lunch place we had been to a while back, so we turned in that direction, but at the last minute I decided the scenic route would be more fun, especially since we had a little time in hand.

We drove along the coast, admiring the blue sky, the hardy walkers and the shell sculpture on the beach, as we approached the next little town. My husband started reminiscing about family holidays taken there, and as we rounded the bend I spotted a line of cars parked outside a pub.

'Shall we try there?' I found myself asking. We easily found a parking place, and as we walked through the garden to the front door we encountered a young woman with two dogs. My husband is fascinated by dogs and she was happy to talk to him about her two.

That was the beginning of a delightful lunch. Serendipity is one word for it. Coincidence another. But I don't think so. I call it Providence and am very grateful. So much better than the struggles of Mrs Fix-it!

Prayer

Thank you, Lord God, for how amazingly you look after us. Help us to be more aware of your loving hand guiding us and protecting us and providing for us.

Self-care suggestion

The key word is 'surrender'. Giving up the 'I must be in charge' can be hard, but it makes a huge difference. Try it!

36

Tears

---•◦•---

Those who sow with tears will reap with songs of joy.

(Psalm 126.5)

Hot tears were pouring down my face. Not the carer's kind – that rush of hopelessness, frustration, overwhelming grief – but hot tears all the same.

The cause? Onions. Today being an outing day, I needed something comforting to come home to. And what is more comforting that a pot of home-made soup? So on with the apron and begin chopping. Remembering my mother-in-law's recipe for leek and potato soup, I prepped the leeks and a couple of cloves of garlic, then set to on an onion.

It was a very fierce onion and in moments my eyes were weeping, my nose running – and of course with both hands oniony and garlicky, trying to get at my handkerchief wasn't easy!

An hour later, the tears are long gone. The soup smells heavenly and will be just perfect with good bread when I get home.

And isn't this our story? We all have tears, but when we look back on our lives, it's not the tears we remember so much as the good times. The happy times. And even at this stage, we can have happy times to enjoy and treasure. That's what I'm hoping for today.

They say you can't make an omelette without breaking a few eggs. Well, you can't make a pot of leek and potato soup without chopping onions and producing floods of tears. Likewise, you can't get through life without some sorrow and suffering, but we are promised strength to carry on. And if we are followers of Christ, a happy ending where there will be no more tears at all!

Prayer

Lord Jesus, give us your strength and comfort to see us through the sad and difficult times. Help us to trust you and know that one day there will be an end to tears; that one day you will personally wipe the tears from our eyes.

Self-care suggestion

My motto tends to be 'When in doubt/misery, make soup'. I'd recommend it to anyone, but what's your stand-by? Make sure you have some ready when you need it!

37

September songs

———◆◆◆———

Let us run with perseverance the race marked out for us.

(Hebrews 12.1b)

I'm watching the folk on the beach this sunny September afternoon. They're different from the summer visitors. This crowd is made up of people at either end of the happy family spectrum: young couples with tiny babies or noisy toddlers, now that school has started again, and at the other end the cheerful, fit, tanned men enjoying the sunshine with their long-time comfortable wives.

As I watch, eating my ice cream after today's outing with my husband, I try to fight the rising emotions: loneliness, sorrow at the loss of my marriage, the shattering of our dreams for a happy retirement together. It all seems worse when I see these happy couples. And, let me admit it, I also feel envy. And anger at the unfairness of it all. Bad feelings. Oh, and self-pity in spades!

But then I look more closely and I see one man valiantly struggling to get to his deckchair, only one leg working because of a massive stroke. And there's another man shuffling behind his wife and the couple they always go on holiday with – the tell-tale shuffle of dementia.

Not everyone is fine and dandy. Many are struggling and suffering. This is life. This is ageing. As my mother-in-law said often, 'If they'd told us this is what ageing is like, we wouldn't have signed up for it!'

But this is where we are. Some days are tougher than others, but that doesn't have to destroy our quality of life. Like the tree that grows strong and deeply rooted in a windy area while another in a sheltered place comes crashing down at the first hint of a storm, our struggles and suffering can make us stronger – and able to find the good in what we're going through.

If, like me, you were an at-home carer for a while before your loved one moved into residential care, you *know* that you're much more of a person than you were before all this started. You've grown and got stronger, more resourceful than you ever thought possible.

Well seasoned. Like good timber. That's us!

Prayer

Loving Lord, hold us in your embrace when we feel lonely and sad. Renew our strength and resource us, that we may continue valiantly to the finishing line.

Self-care suggestion

There are days when I can't face the happy couples who make my loneliness more painful. But it's not good for me to isolate myself. I know that some people avoid me now, as though dementia were infectious and they don't want their beloved husbands to catch it. But there are others who understand, those who ask sensible questions – and even sometimes remember to ask how I am. When you feel down and lonely, seek out the people you know will understand (and avoid the ones who don't).

38

Thank you

Give thanks in all circumstances; for this is God's will for you in
Christ Jesus. (1 Thessalonians 5.18)

There are good days. Good visits. Moments when the fog lifts and the
person you knew and loved is there again, smiling at you, knowing
who you are. And even when he doesn't, you can still find something
to enjoy.

No? I can hear the rumbles of disagreement, but I'm sticking to
my position. Of course, I've been there in that miserable gloomy
place, where it all seems so horrible and there's no light at the end
of the tunnel because you cannot bear to let yourself even think about
it. When dragging yourself dutifully in for the visit is almost more
than you can bear.

But that's when you need to count your blessings the most.
Gratitude has an amazing transformative quality. At the end of the
day – even after a disastrous visit where everything went wrong and
he got upset (or you got upset) – try to find three things to say thank
you to God for.

Your heart may at first rebel, but stick with it. To start with, you may
grudgingly acknowledge the roof over your head, a clean dry bed,
food in your tummy . . . but persevere and from the back cupboards
of your mind may creep some happy thoughts. Maybe the visit wasn't
all bad? Maybe just being able to go there and get through the visit
is something to give thanks for?

And maybe there are memories you want to say thank you
for? Memories of happier times. Yes, they may make you cry,
but maybe that's good in itself. Good tears are something to be
grateful for.

Making a habit of gratitude, of looking every day for three things
to say thank you sincerely to God for, will change how you feel about

your day, so you go to sleep more peacefully and with a little more happiness than you realized was there.

And the door will be open for a little more happiness, more things to say thank you for, tomorrow.

Prayer

Thank you, Lord God, for your love and your care and your provision for us.

Self-care suggestion

You might like to get a little notebook and use it to write down, each night before you go to sleep, the three things you want to say thank you for. If you do it every day, by the end of the year there will be over 1,000. Isn't that wonderful? You'll have had over 1,000 things to say thank you for! (Thanks for this idea to the wonderful Ann Voskamp, author of *One Thousand Gifts: A Dare to Live Fully Right Where You Are*, published by Zondervan (2011), and her inspirational blog, <www.aholyexperience.com>.)

Index